AF256149

The Garden Door

*Words and Images
from Paths New and Trodden*

Camilla C Saufley

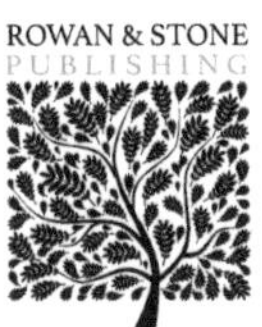

ROWAN & STONE
PUBLISHING

Cover and book design by Camilla C Saufley

First Edition
ISBN 978-1-7357309-0-5

Rowan & Stone Publishing
PO BOX 561
Forest Knolls, CA 94933

email: info@rowanandstone.com
website: www.rowanandstone.com

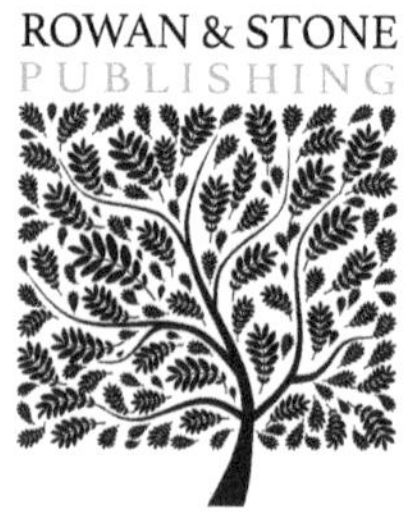

Cover photo: Ridgetop. Inverness, California

For Jeanie Kortum

who showed me the path home

The Dance of Ink

I want to write my heart
that every word might heal it
that every phrase might be a gift
of light
and grace.

I want to write my spirit
that these words might give us wings
and with ink and paper
we might fly
in rains of compassion.

I want to write my soul
eternal and yet
here we are.
Each of us tied
to this mortal coil
this fleshy mass
that animates us and gives us speech
        and song
        and dance.

And to this body, a thank you
a love letter.
You carried me through
giving life to touch
and in touch, a pathway
back to the heart.

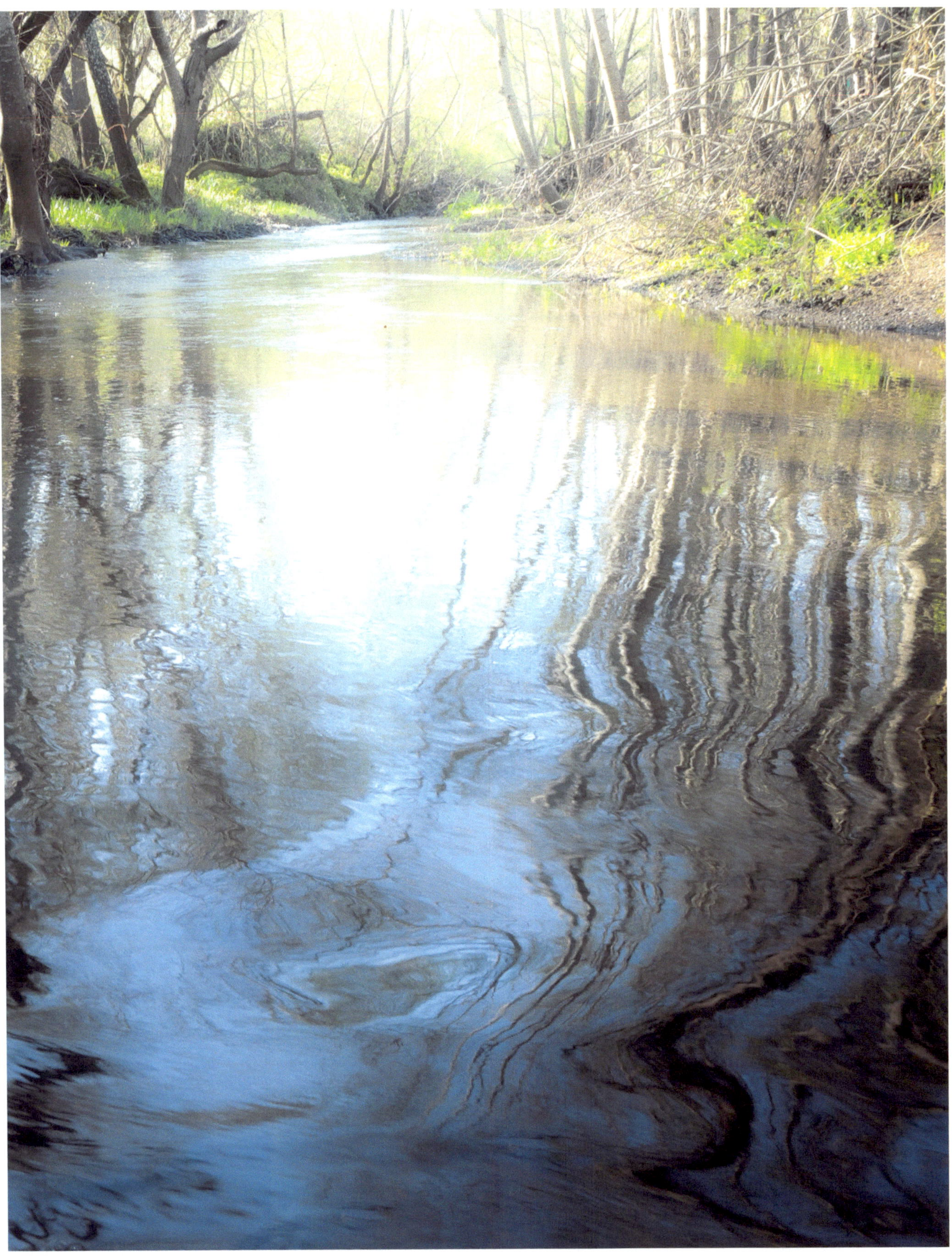

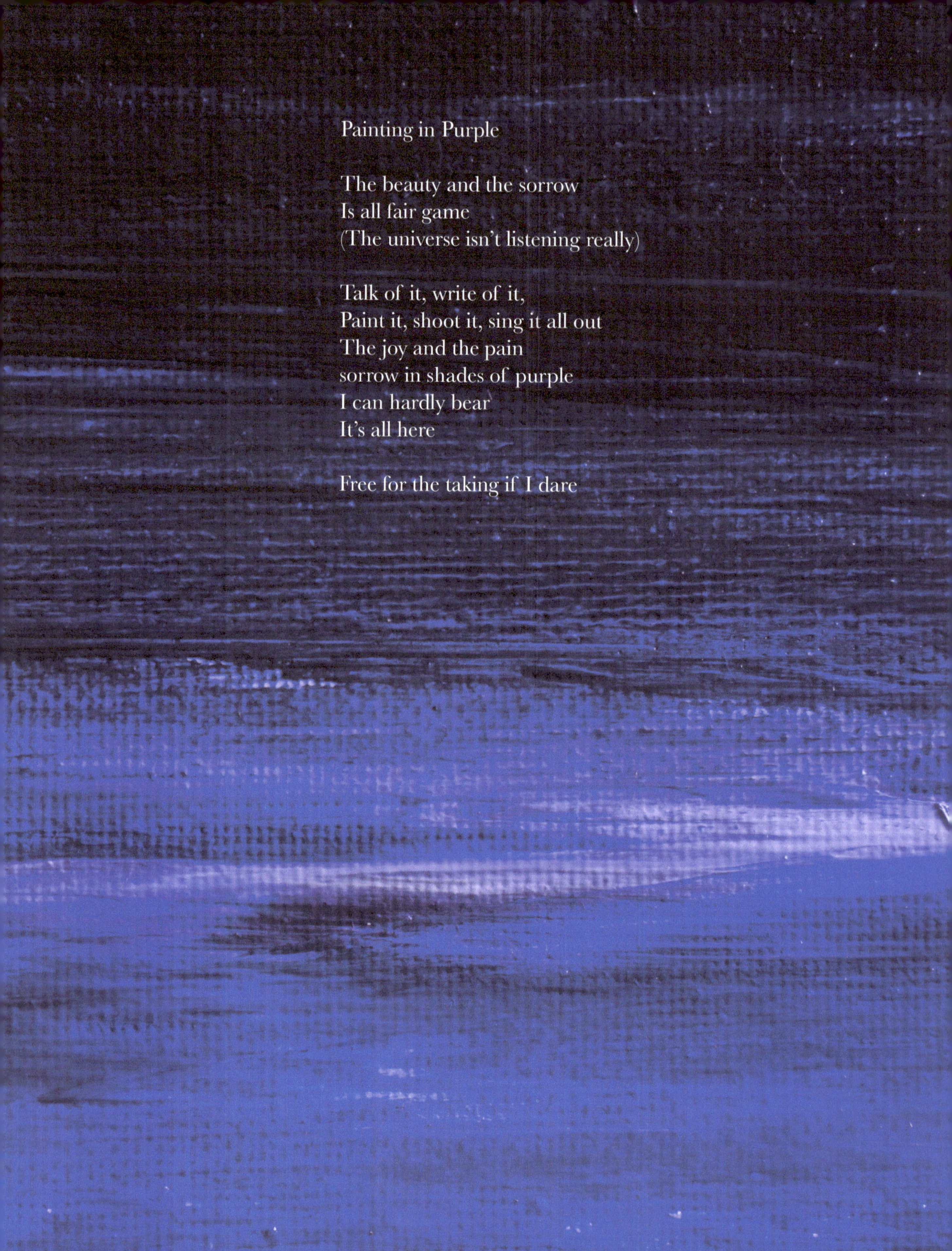

Painting in Purple

The beauty and the sorrow
Is all fair game
(The universe isn't listening really)

Talk of it, write of it,
Paint it, shoot it, sing it all out
The joy and the pain
sorrow in shades of purple
I can hardly bear
It's all here

Free for the taking if I dare

To Your Garden Door

Sleep you elude
while the nest
is so warm
I nestle in
and such comfort
there is
and yet
      rattle
            rattle
                  rattle
at the mind's door
Breathing
and breathing
and slowly sinking
but never to
your deepening floor

Take me drifting
and dreaming
of sweet things

To your garden door

The Treehouse

She was right
every word of it
Sitting in that tiny room
on a soft chair covered in doillies
and pillows
and a headless doll

She was right
The path forward
is lined with cobblestones
Crafted from pigment
and sound
Every step lit
with the things I've given away
the places I lost direction to.
The destination is unknown
but the path is shown

Whoever meets me on this road
shall know what I know
The magic
and the math
of the equation
she gave back

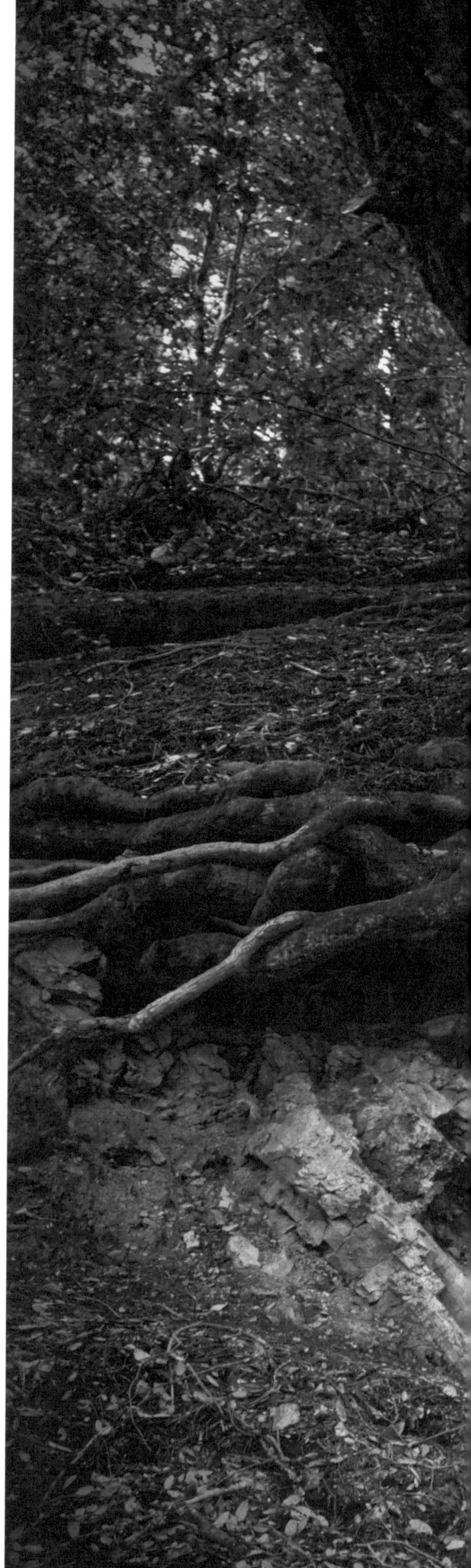

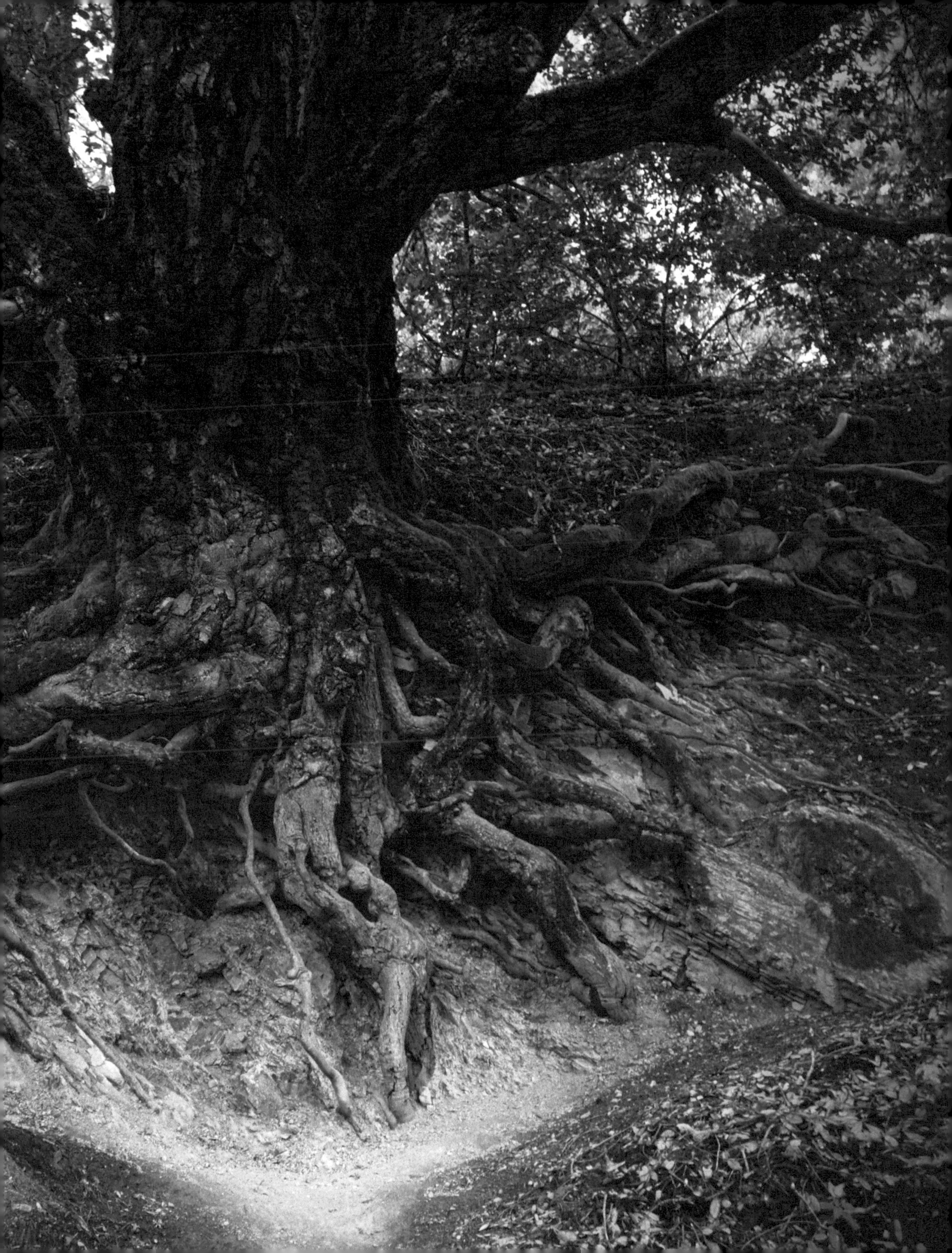

Kauai

Shimmering green
fronds alight with a menagerie
of feathered callings
The constant surround
of ocean as it laps
crashes against the shore
Thoughts
Emotions
crashing against the shores of my mind
My heart

A din
          To a roar
A gentle passing
               Lap, lap
To a raging, ripping hurricane

Tearing at foundations of
my stony shore
Pulling ancient fossils
of memory
               and pattern
Those things that can no longer stay

Torn out by this raging storm
Breaking down shoreline
that has stood watch
over the tender interior
The meadows of heart
The forest – that sanctuary
to the most sacred parts
Tearing down
Stone by stone
Fossil by fossil
until the storm passes
and sets them free

To drift and sink
Into the sea.

Rán

Trickling down like a silent spring.
If someone had been kinder with his heart,
he would be kinder to his own.
Kinder to mine.

I walked miles to swim in seas of peace.
When you become the ocean,
there are no waves.

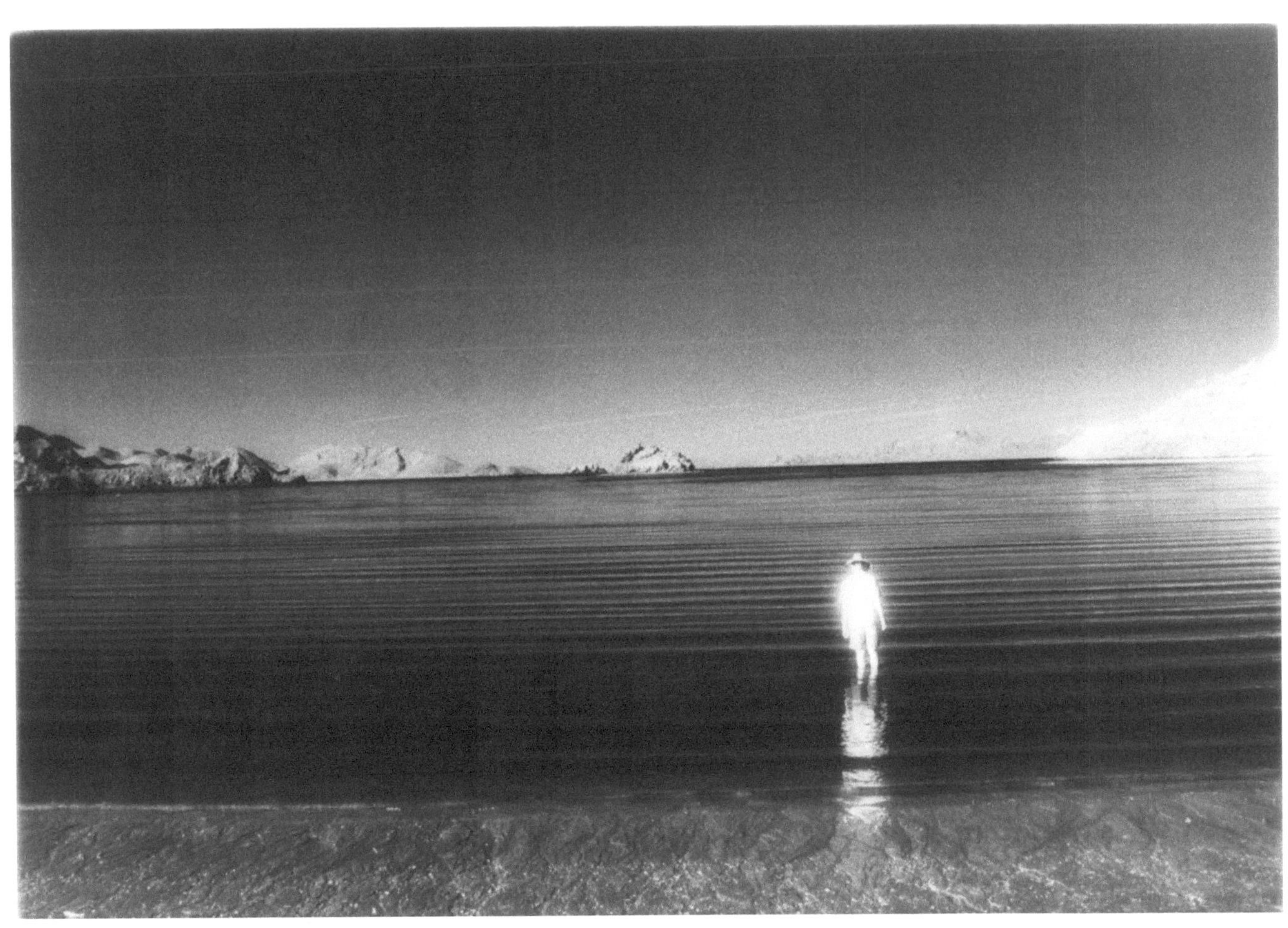

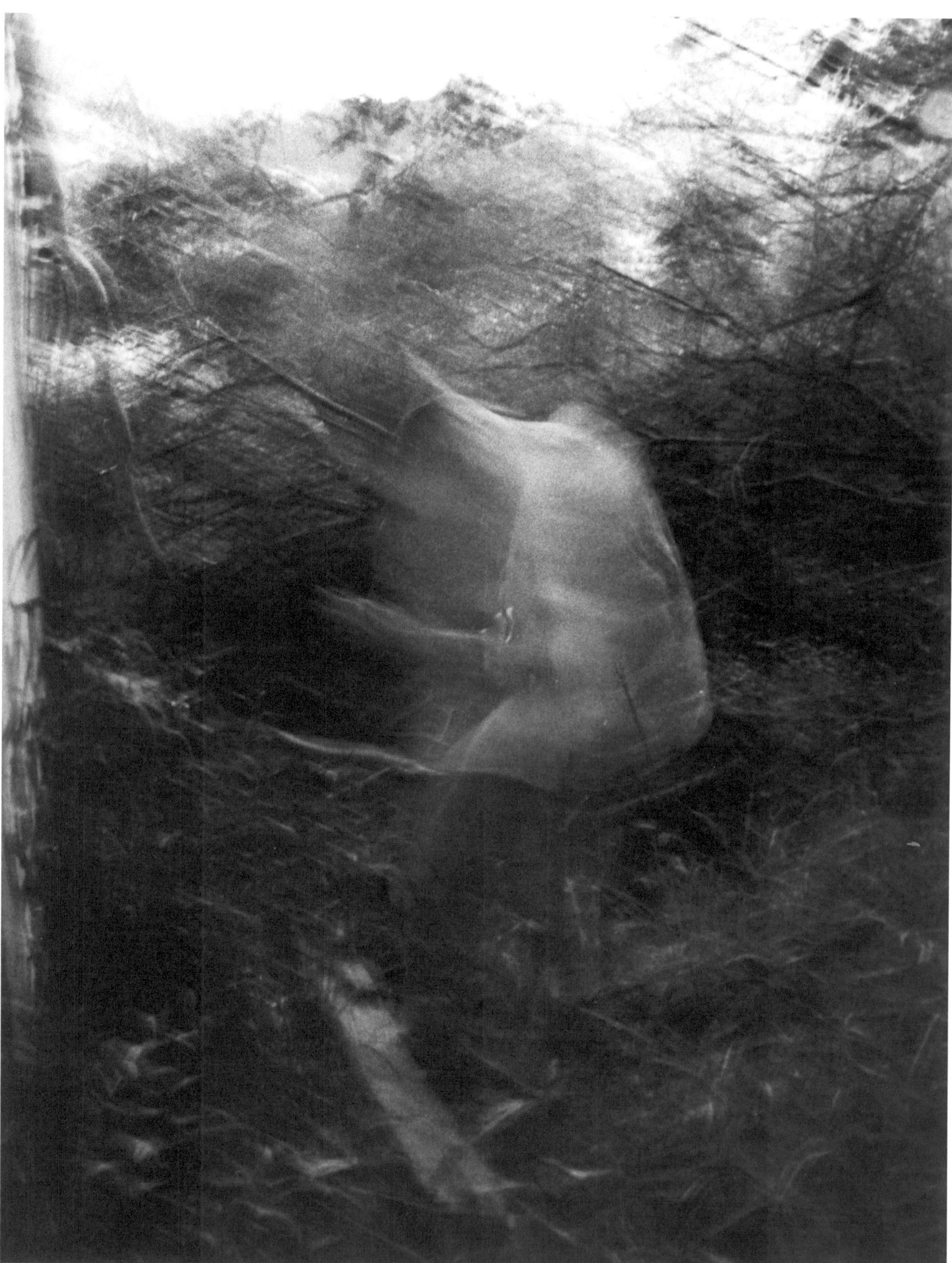

Midnight, Christmas Day

The bells are ringing
Calling
Rise up and pray

Rain falling on the window pane
Brings rhythm to midnight
Wish I could lie in these sheets with you
Watching leaves fall
The last of the few
Dark skies and late nights
A world away where I long to stay

Kind one
He's a kind one
Ever there day to day
Then it was Londontown
Holding me gently
as I climbed into
the impossibly tiny bed
One moment of warmth
Comfort, kindness
A light in the fog
Tiniest hope
of what will one day come shining back
And the bells are ringing out

May the bells keep ringing
Calling me back
While black trees dance
with amber leaves
My heart knows
My spirit sees

I saw your ghost down
crowded Christmas streets
I keep walking,
Heartlight torching
Those deepening shadows
where you hide

Until your ghost
will haunt me no more.

Anticipation

Stillness of Sunday
as gentle as a stream.
Even woodpecker
is late to rise.
It's as if the world
is waiting.
Quietly.
For what?

Foxglove reaches higher
like a towering castle
for a faerie queen.
Dew drops settle
like diamonds.
And in it all
Stillness.
Quiet.

Freedom from the need to know
what comes next.

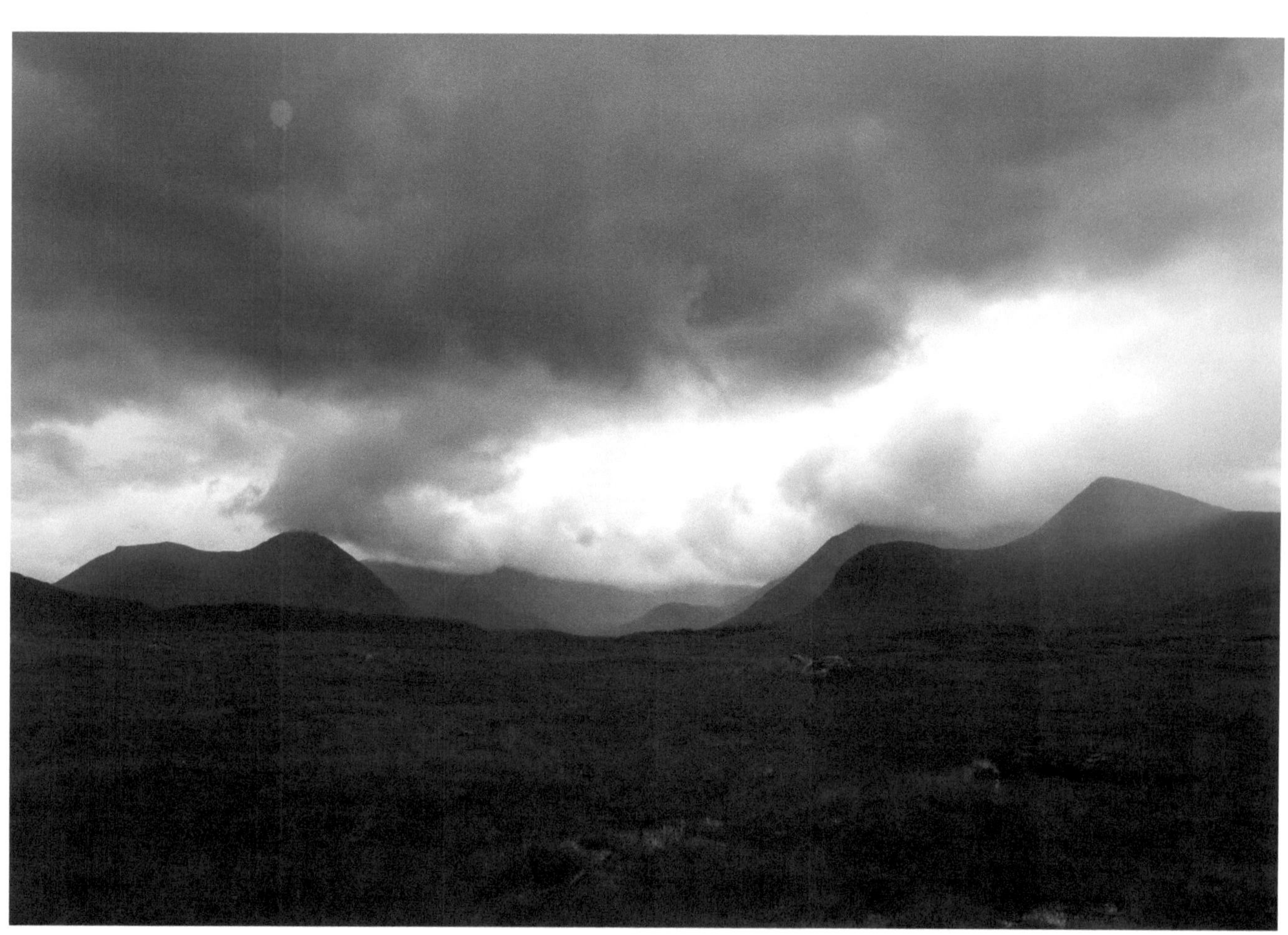

On the Eve of St Valentine's Day

Sunny days
Have faded to grey
I've no obligation
To say
          Or do
          Or be
Something sunny.

Some days I want to watch
The icy cold light
dance across forested hillsides.
Silhouettes of rock forms
and soft hill shapes
that flatten
as the day turns from dog to wolf.

And a single
bright star
that used to call your name
but now calls someone else's
Longitudes away
He looks up
and knows it too.

I burned the last of you
in the fire last night.
On the eve of St Valentine's Day.

Nuns Canyon

Nuns Canyon Creek
running deep
Deeper still the season.

The goldening of leaves
high above in a cyan sky
Listening to ripples on stone
She said "We never step into
the same river twice"
Soothing, the sound of water
calls of blue jay
and woodpecker.

The woods behind the house
still charred and black
from the devastation
and destruction
sometimes required
for new shoots to rise.

A black skeletal forest.

A reminder of what must die
to be reborn.

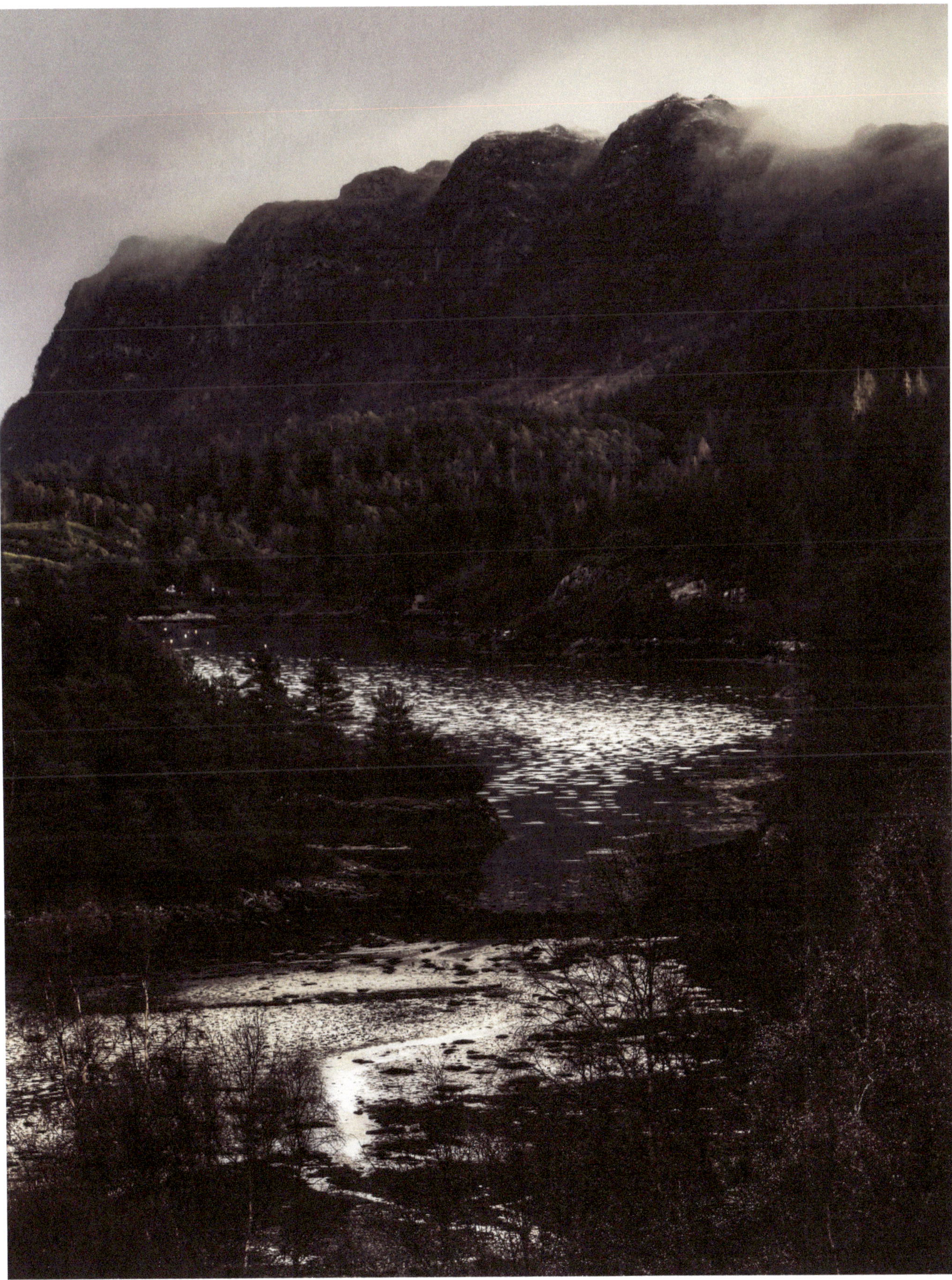

Mountain Eyes

Perspective is everything.
A towering mountain range
A vast open sea
Miles that look like minutes
and me – here for a blink of an eye
in the shadow of the Great One.

So grand seem the things
we fret about
The burdens we carry
the anxious thoughts of yesterday
and the next day
and the next.

But the mountain – she reminds me
of all she has seen
and I and my worries
are but the beat of a butterfly wing.

Best not to waste any more precious time.

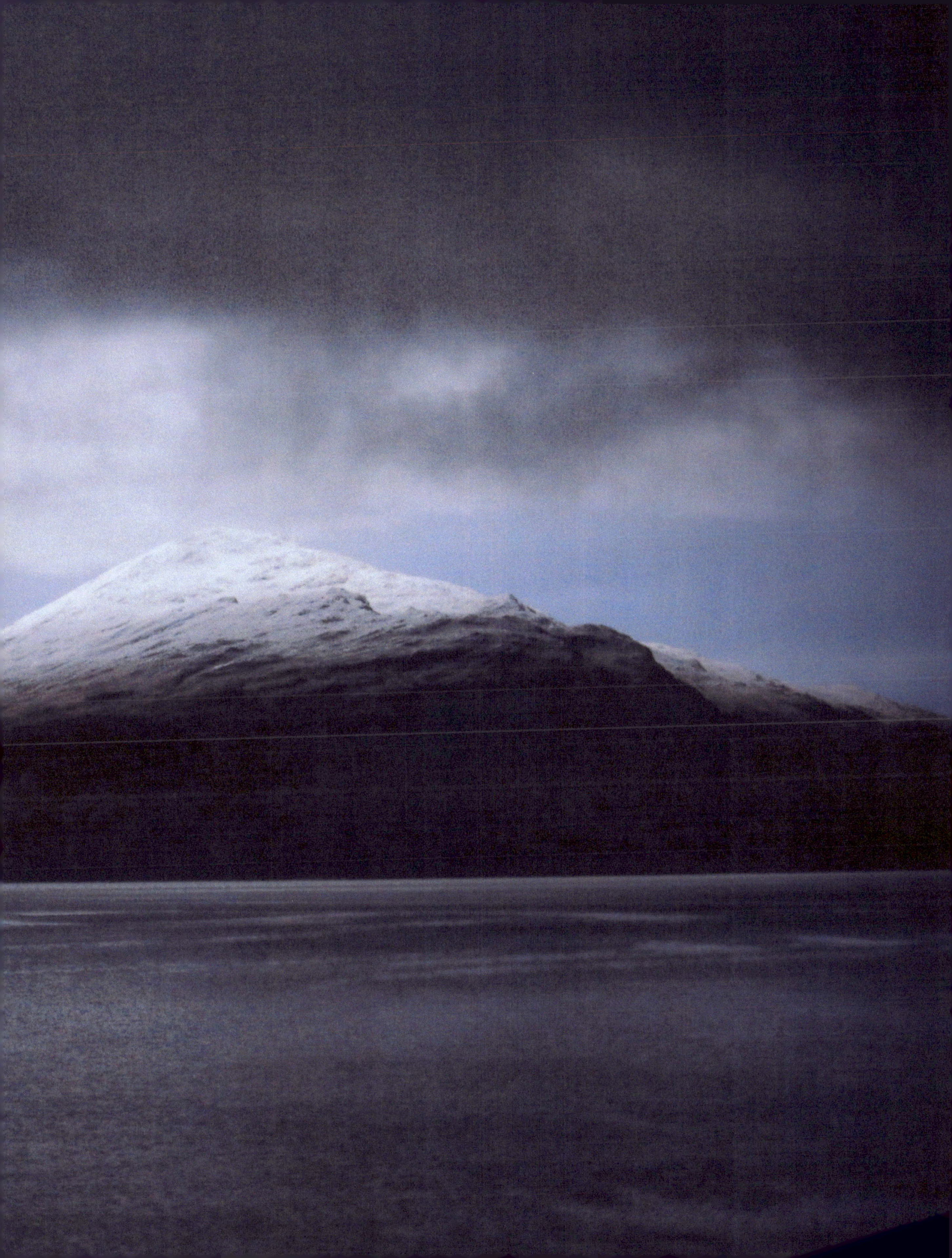

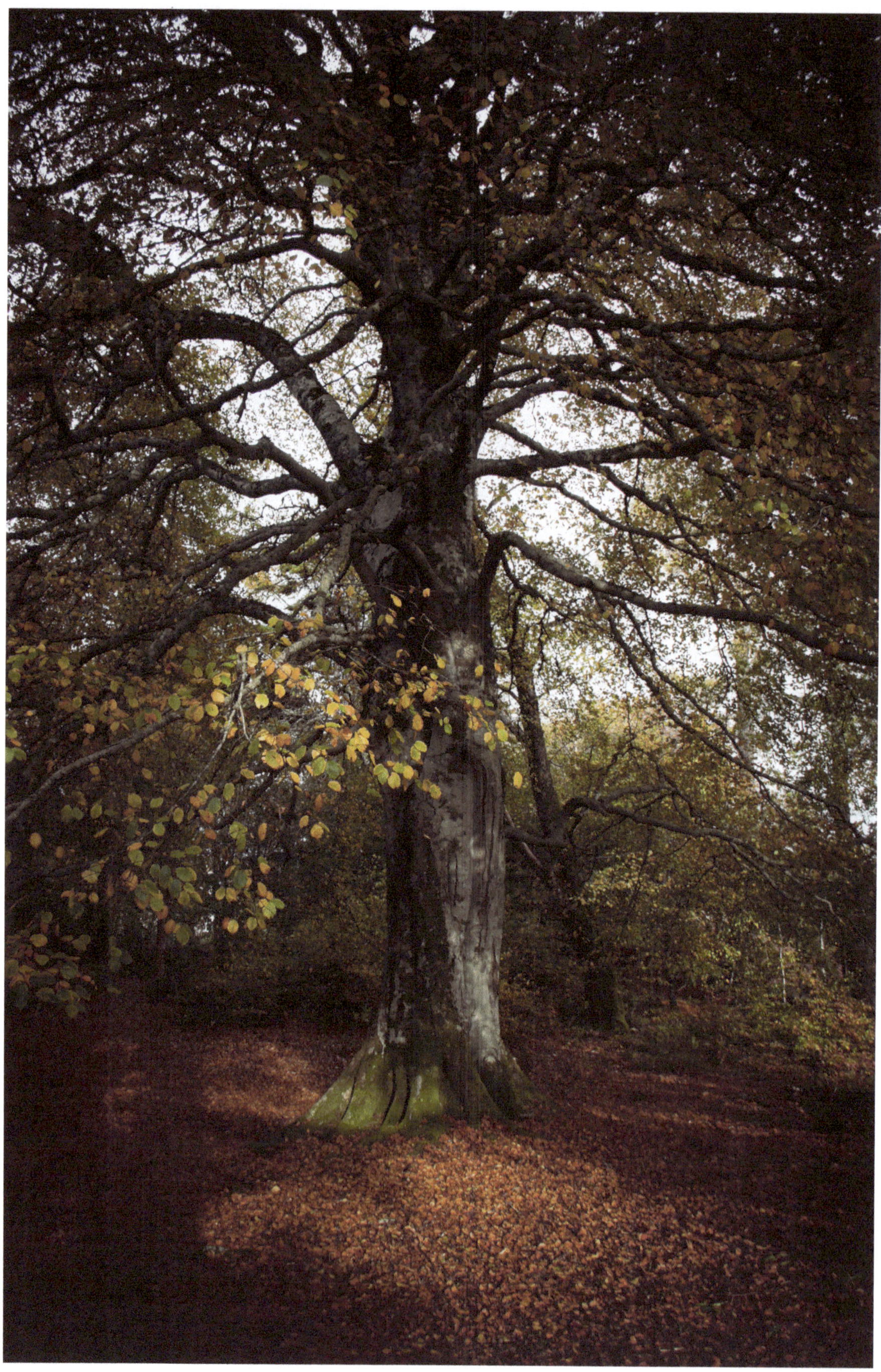

For Luther Burbank

For this moment
I sit
in the shade of your birch tree
whose leaves whisper
the secrets of the sea
to the West

And as apples ripen
And warm in the sun
I feel the stillness
And it is all exactly as it was.

A dream.

The Road Out of Town

Yellow bathes the earthen floor
Dancing lights
shimmer and pour
through ancient limbs.

I'm here again
among the seeds you've sown
So many have we gone and come
to light upon your dusty row.

As yellow flowers dance in the wind.

In the Cottage

Quiet words
evasive eyes
your stories lie
deep inside

We talk through song
Notes our words
until at last
the light pours out
shining through.
We light and dance,
we sing and pray

Tomorrow never comes
it's always today

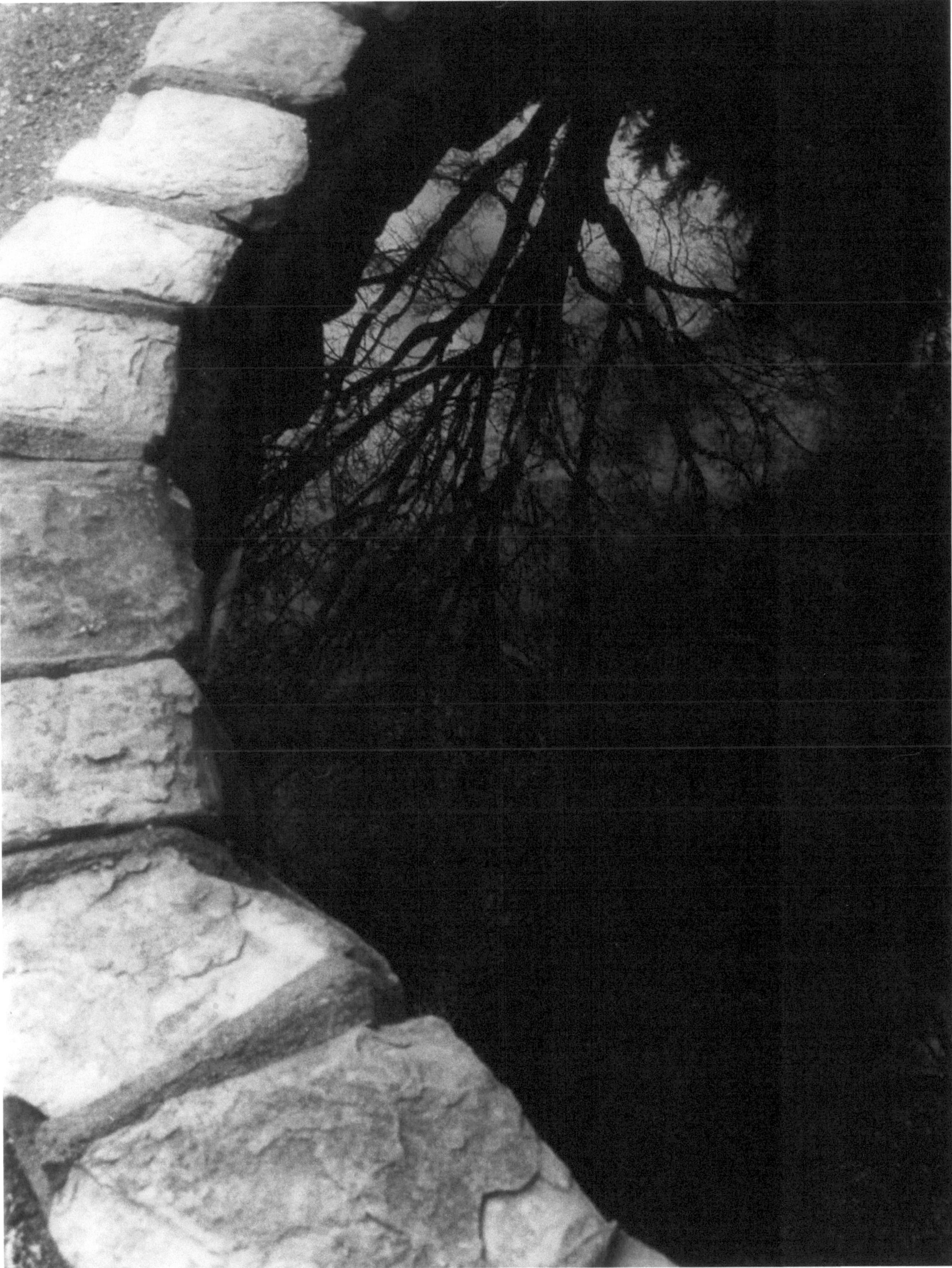

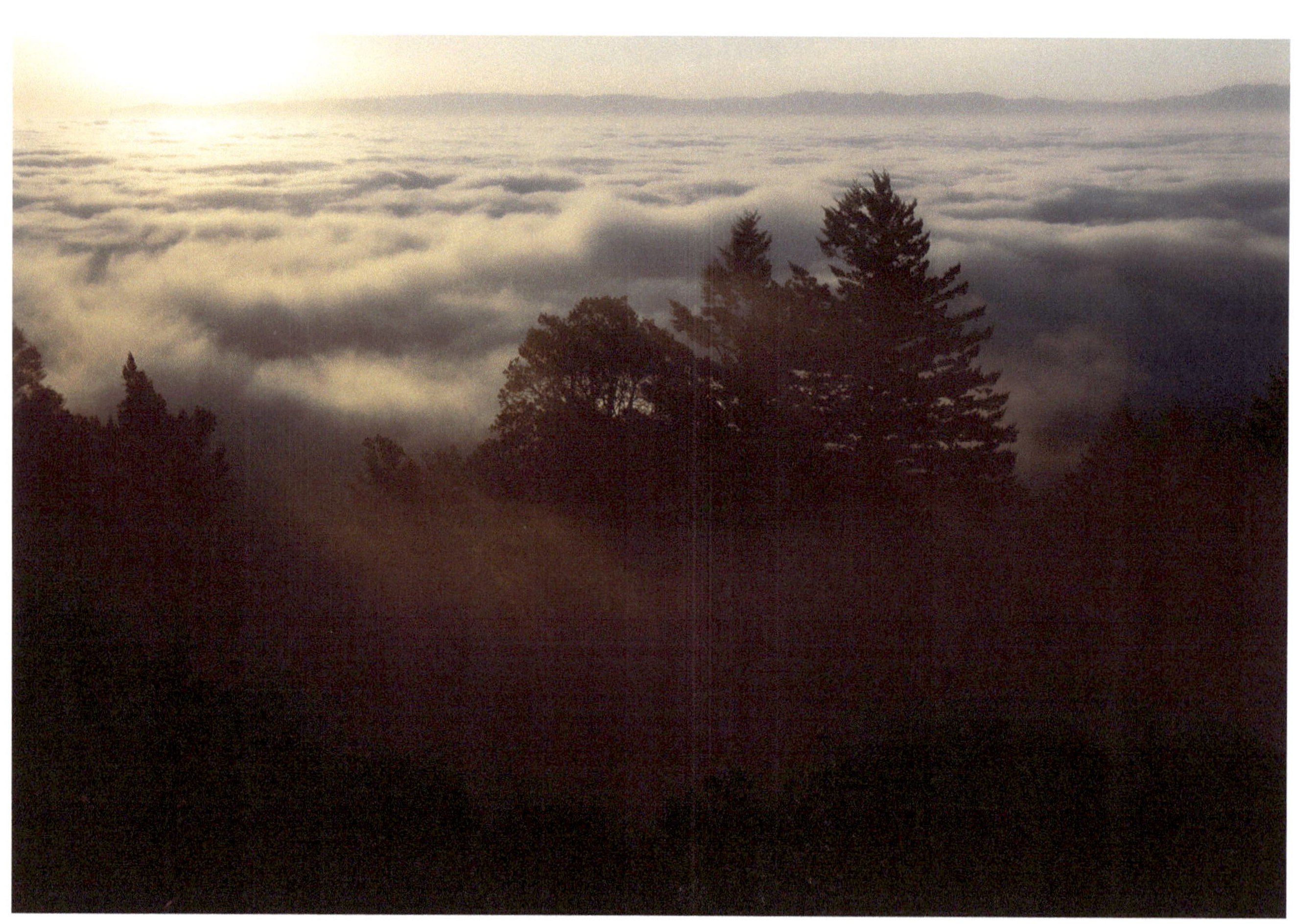

Pescadero

Winding roads
of memory's map
past tall trees
still strong
after ages of swaying
in Pacific winds
Past the red barn
and creekside taverns
wood clad cabins
and fields of rusted cars
shaded pools
of dusty summer camp
creek dips

And a winding path
up darkened duff
I couldn't see the top
but I remember what's there
The place we said we would meet
in the afterlife
          (if such things were possible)
A clearing
so green
beneath towering redwood trees.
I don't remember the details entirely
nor do I think I could find it again
But I remember
that you loved me then.

Jon and the Sleeping Lady

So many greens!
Shades of spring
That lie upon
Your sleeping side

I've stood here before
Maybe fifty times
Hearing the woodpecker's song
On winding paths
Where chocolate lilies grow

And dreams.
I came here first
with he who is not here
          (no it was alone)
I would stand upon
this hillside
Paths wandering
to the rushing of sacred springs
that run
deep deep deep
even in summer

This canyon my first escape
from concrete streets
and shimmering towers
To this great
Mother of a Mountain
Always beckoning
for miles around

Here there is a clarity
A freshness
A freedom
Here I watched my
first forested sunsets
as blue gave way to
silver and gold
Marveling at this magic
just a step outside.

It was here
That my love was born
Where my Mother Mountain
became my sanctuary

Summer days that felt so long!
Hot sunshine beating
upon tanned arms
As I set out for
another adventure
A new discovery
          A new view
          And sometimes a hard road.

Once, we reached the top.
Brambles and scratched legs
too impatient to
take the long way round.

It was victory
and you laughed that you'd never walk again
as pounding hillside
beat mercilessly upon
your athlete's knees
I remember each path, each discovery
Alone
and with others
          Only special few

Today a cold wind runs
up this canyon
as swiftly as my
memories come rushing back
All the gifts
this forest has given.
Endless summer days
all rushing back
in the heady scent
of laurel leaves
and the dream
of never going back home.

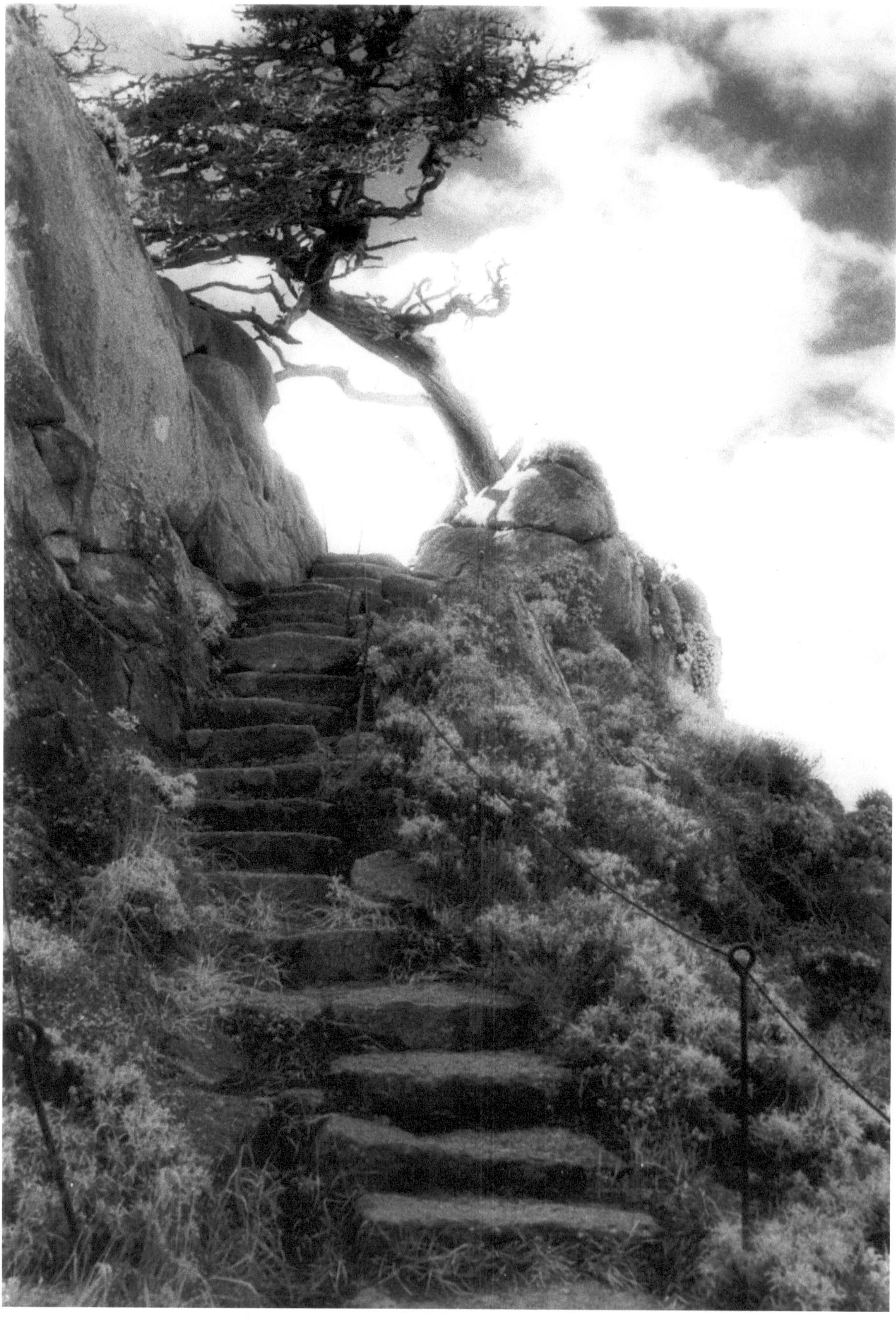

Owl Council

A path not taken
A mystery unfolding
A rustle in the wood
A theatre of magic
Found down a lost path
Walking within a light
Just a sliver
They begin.

Memories dance of those come before
I hear her voice calling them
She's calling but gone again
Wil-o-the-wisp
A voice in the river
A bird's dusky cry
Calling deeply as water
Taken on high
They begin.

Come in child – nothing to fear
Give it all away
like drifting sand
We take it all
and give back
what is meant for you.

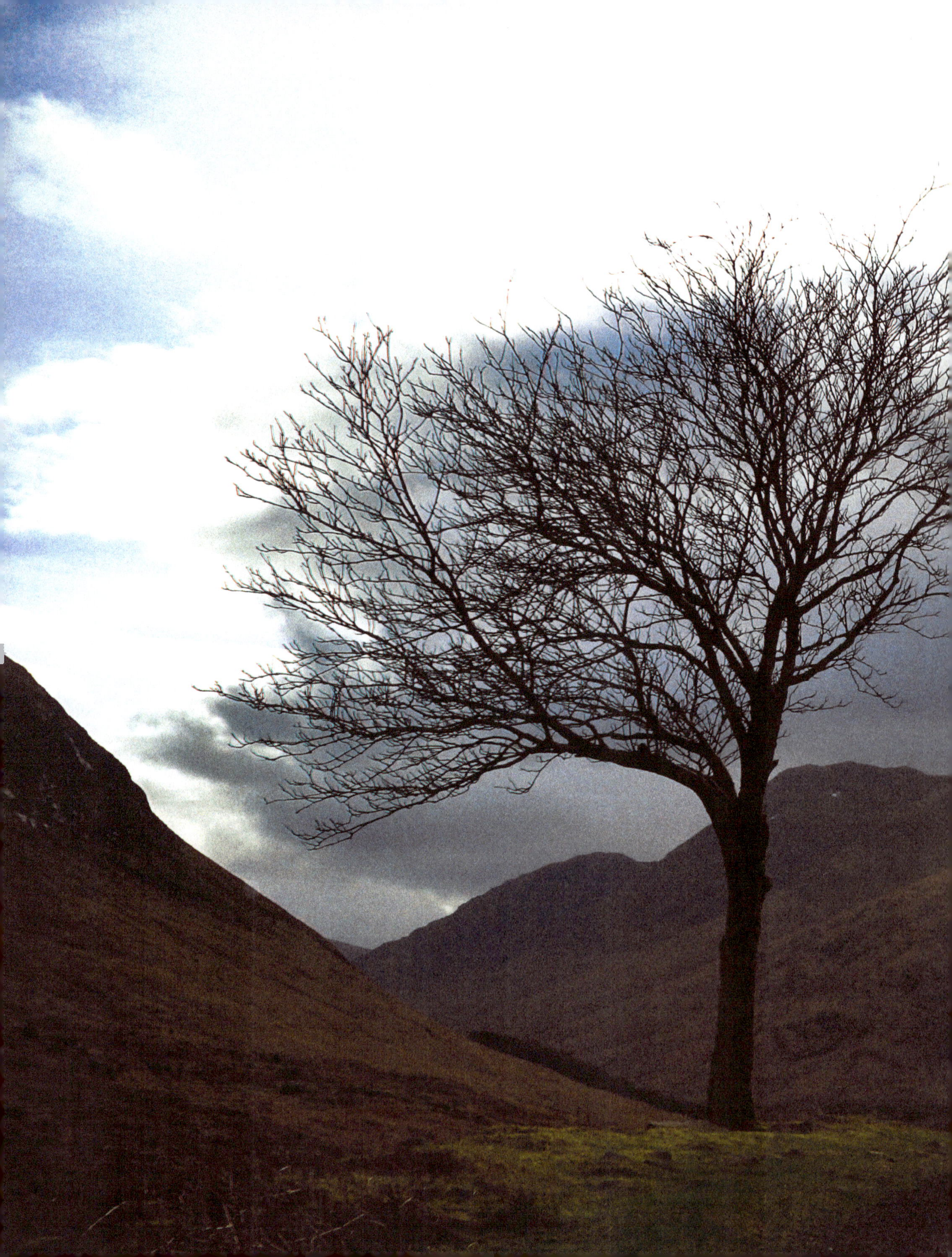

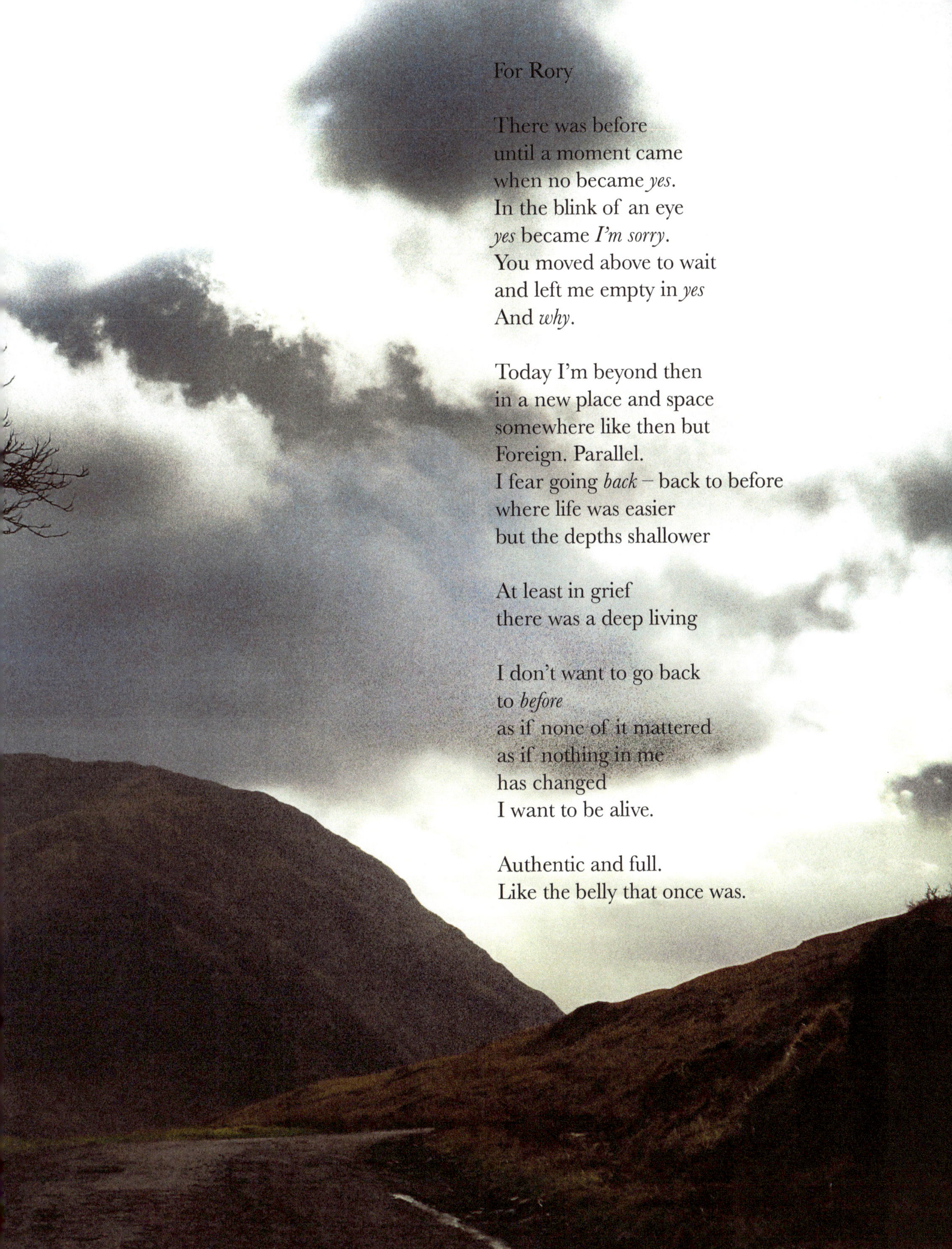

For Rory

There was before
until a moment came
when no became *yes*.
In the blink of an eye
yes became *I'm sorry*.
You moved above to wait
and left me empty in *yes*
And *why*.

Today I'm beyond then
in a new place and space
somewhere like then but
Foreign. Parallel.
I fear going *back* – back to before
where life was easier
but the depths shallower

At least in grief
there was a deep living

I don't want to go back
to *before*
as if none of it mattered
as if nothing in me
has changed
I want to be alive.

Authentic and full.
Like the belly that once was.

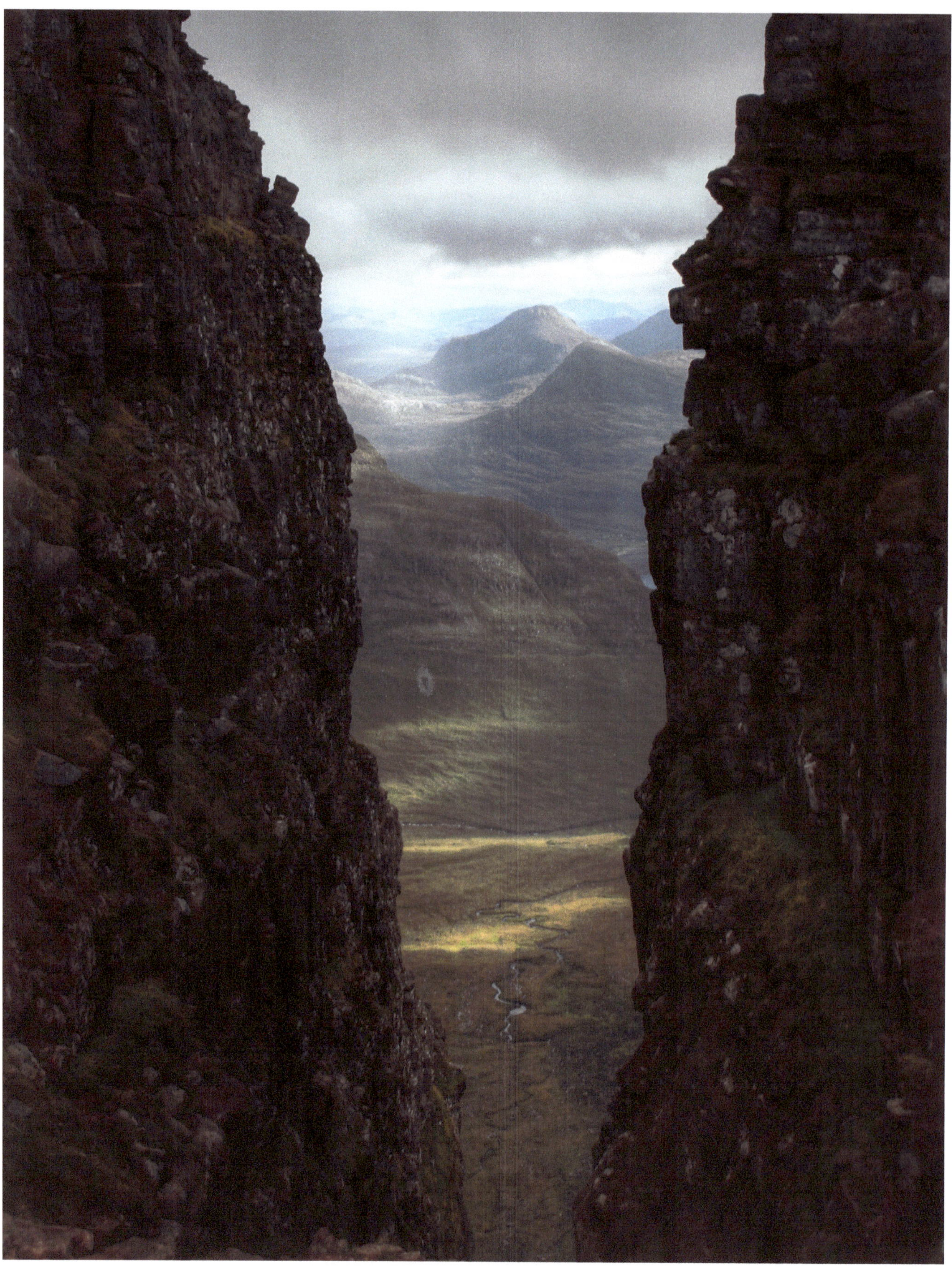

The Gift of Summer's Parting

Eyes open
to soft and heavy.
This morning's light
still hiding behind
old world guardians
who looked this way
long before our hearts
were even a thought.
Stirrings in the air
memories borrowed and lost
and clouds like great exaggerations
bring cold creepings.

Warm winds cannot hide
what lies behind
The gift of summer's parting

As we feel the yearning
of copper pots and hearth
Yellow and gold
Dreams so old
Around us they
gather and nest
and calves lie low in the fading.
Quiet arrives.

Autumn
The introspective one.

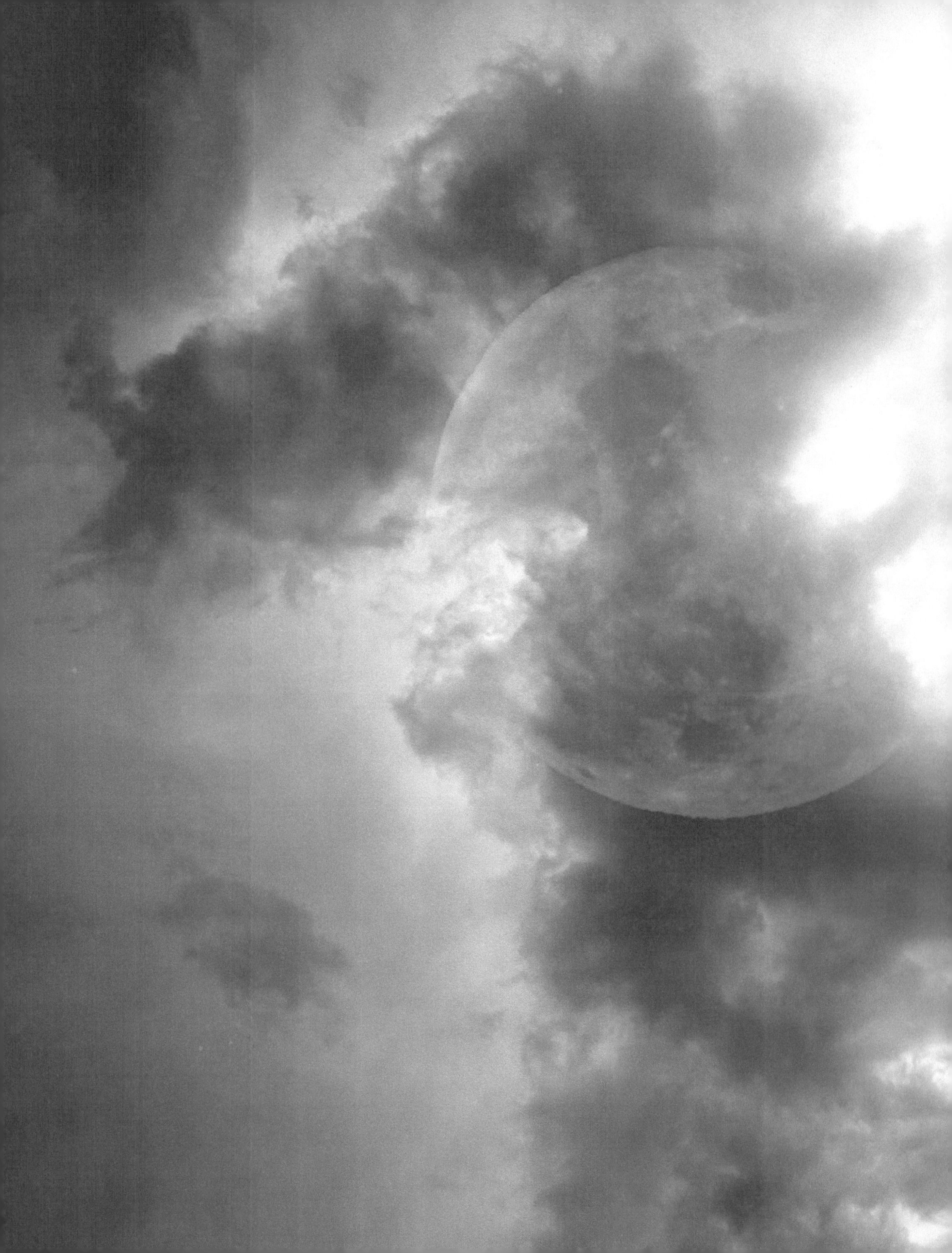

Night Gardening

Hello Moon
I'd forgotten your face
Days since I've seen you
welcoming the rainy veil
that hid your smile
So bright suddenly
rays shining through the ancient oak
while water moves
down the once empty creek bed
A subtle hum
like leaves in the wind
Enough light to dig into the earth
        a hole here
            another there
The fresh forest garden
awake in the wet cool moonlight

I may never garden by day again.

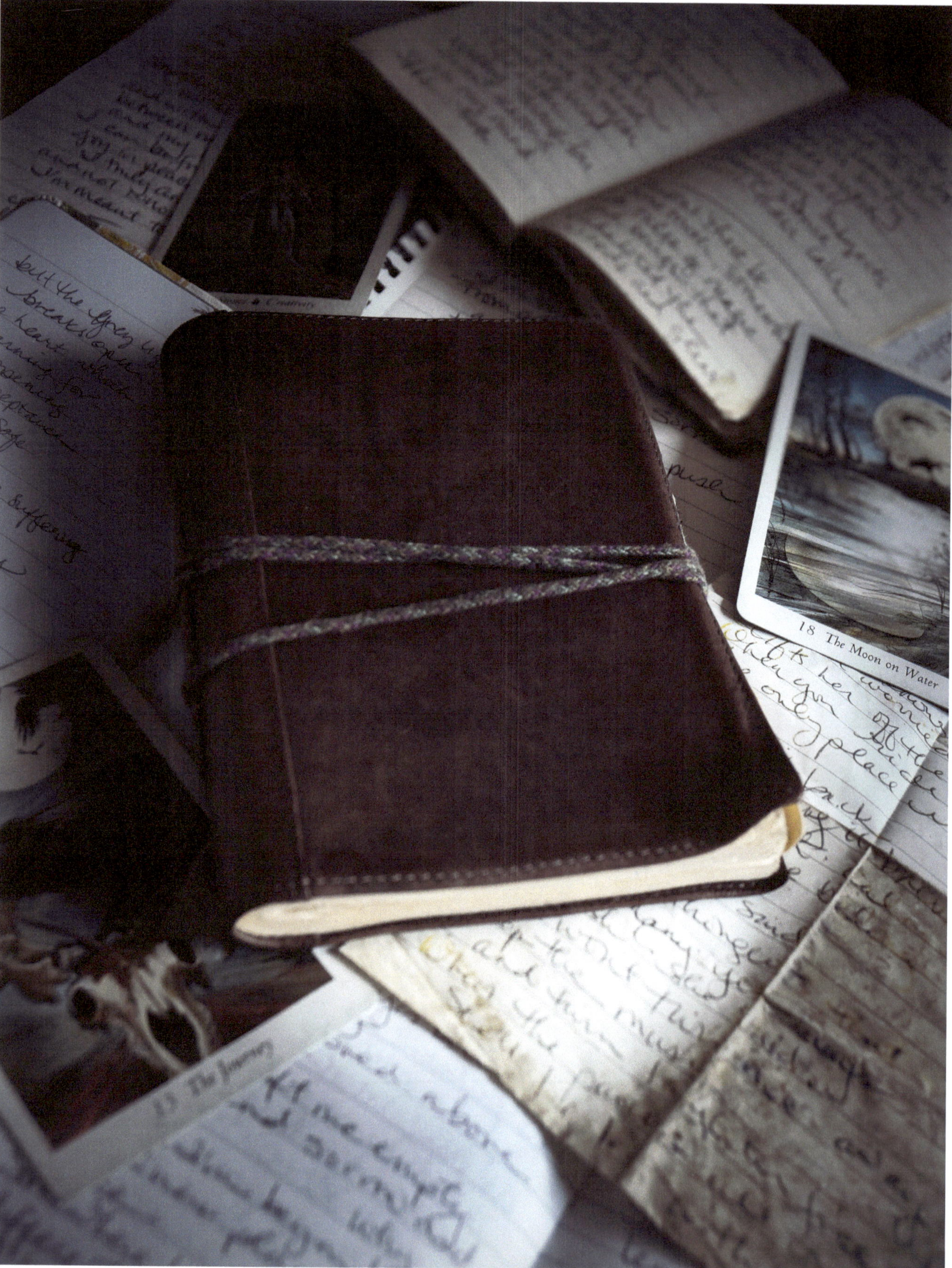
18 The Moon on Water

Glasgow

From sun to grey
Skies darken
as tears fall
Torn from those I love
like the generations
ripped from this land
they called home.

I was born in another
but that does not make it home.

Mountains and Sisters

A moment and a mountain
Rivers and rocks
press against time and memory
Love and acceptance
and a question answered

Who was I before?
Before your veiling clouds
swallowed my time
swallowed my dreams

Ah, but at last I find
when you're a dreamer
dreams never die
They only wait for the right time
to rise and float
and soar again.

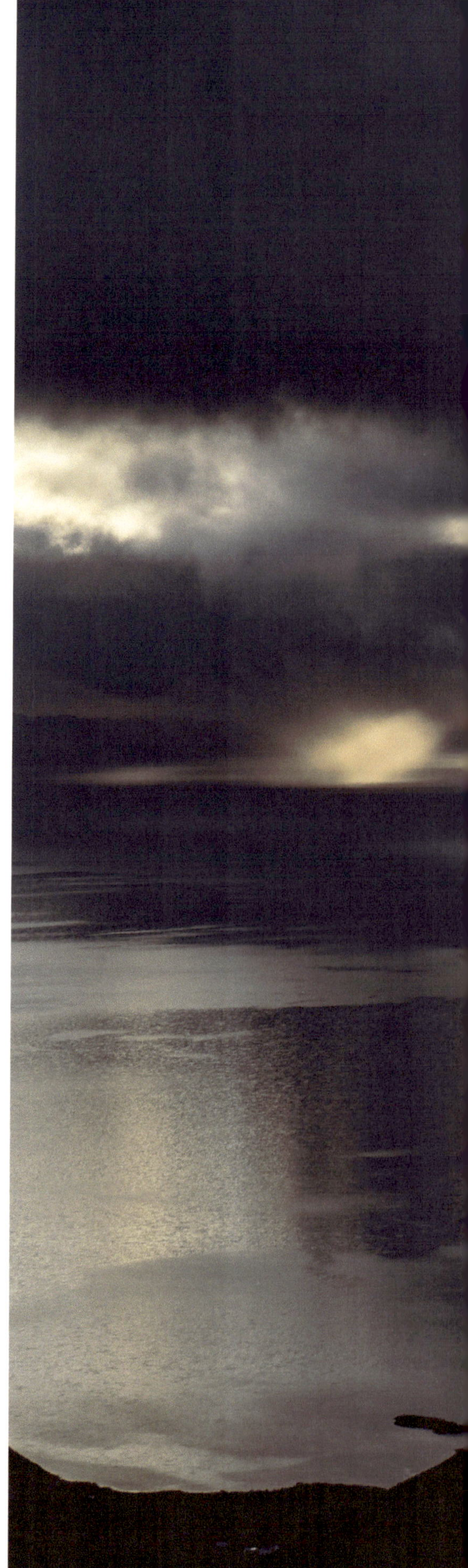

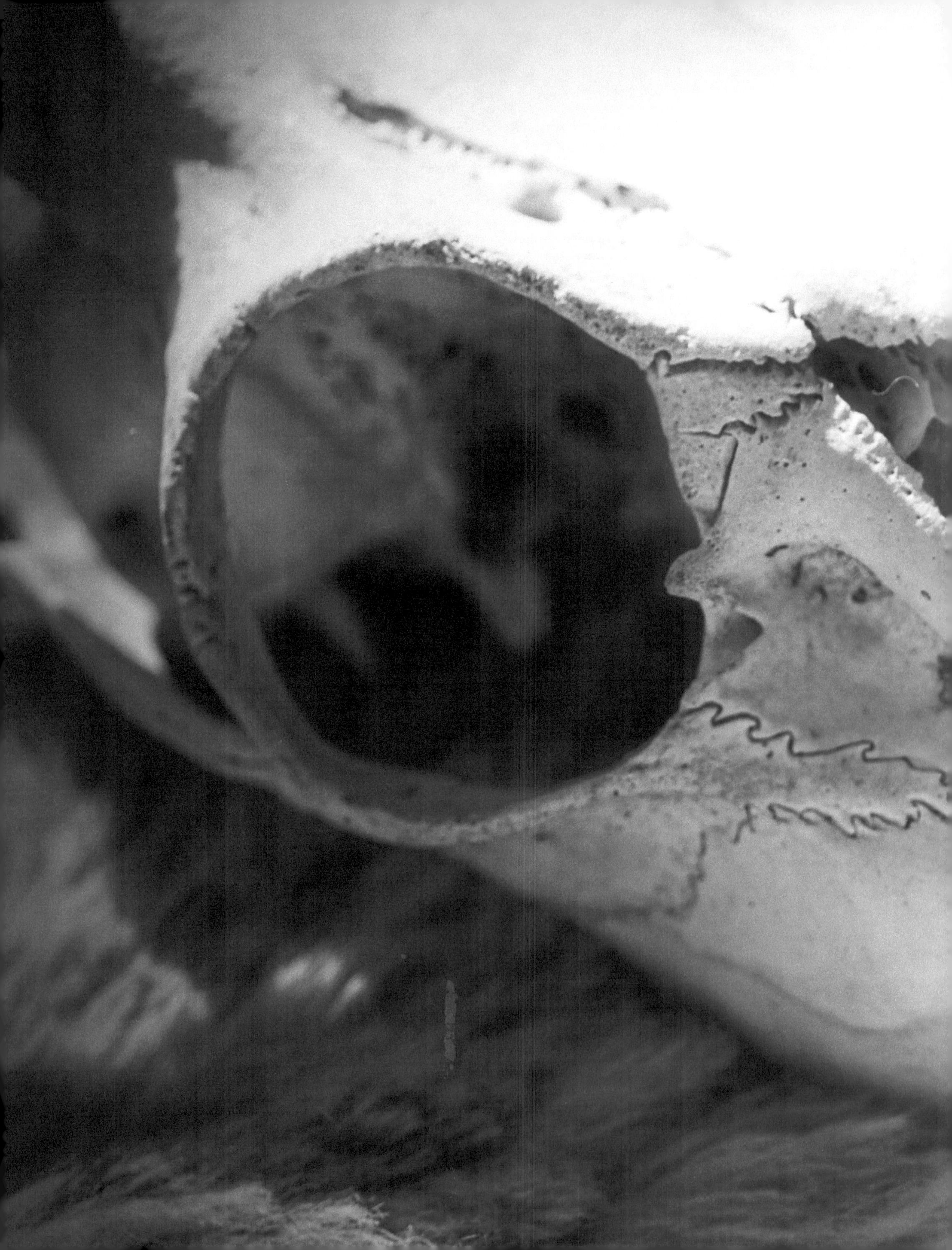

Samsāra

Passing, moving, shifting
lines on a circle
all intertwined
A web woven
not today
or even yesterday
Eternal

I knew you then
when skies turned red
with a power we couldn't understand
Walking beneath
a fading sun
as darkness changed our wonder
to horror

Countless other lives
entwined and well…
here we are again
as each passing day
erases impressions of
ancient tales untold
Until at dusk
our lights fade
one by one
before unfolding again

Who will we be
next time around?

Props

Thank you for this gift of clarity.
This knowledge that I am not defined by you
Nor did you ever deserve
or own my power.
These memories are mine
Not bound in sorrow
with your presence in them
Mine to remember
relish and release
To visit again
reclaiming space and time
in a land that was always mine

In this theatre
you are but an actor
with a part to play.
And now the curtain comes down
The stage remains.
The props will come and go.
But in this theatre
the play has just begun
Again.

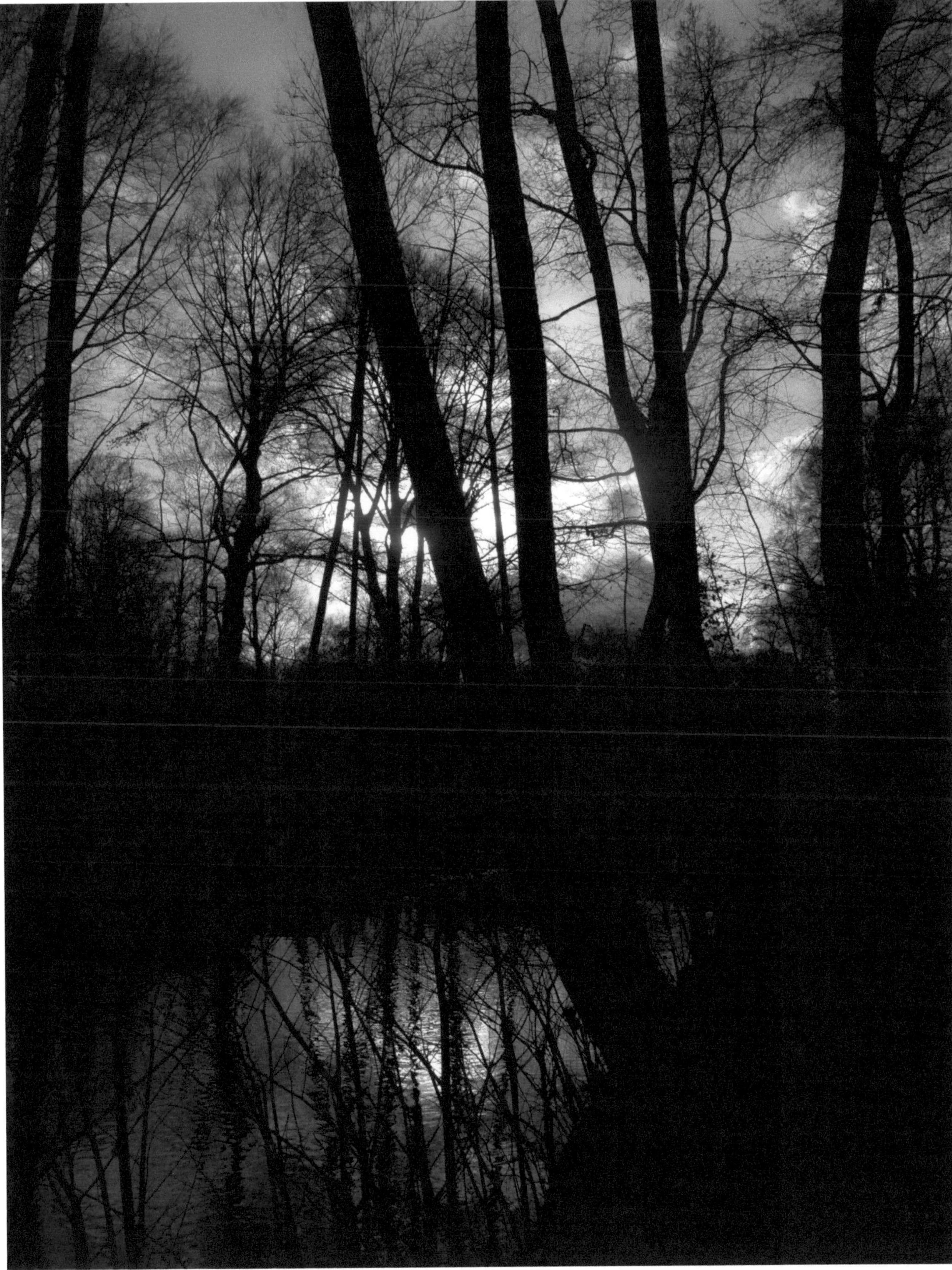

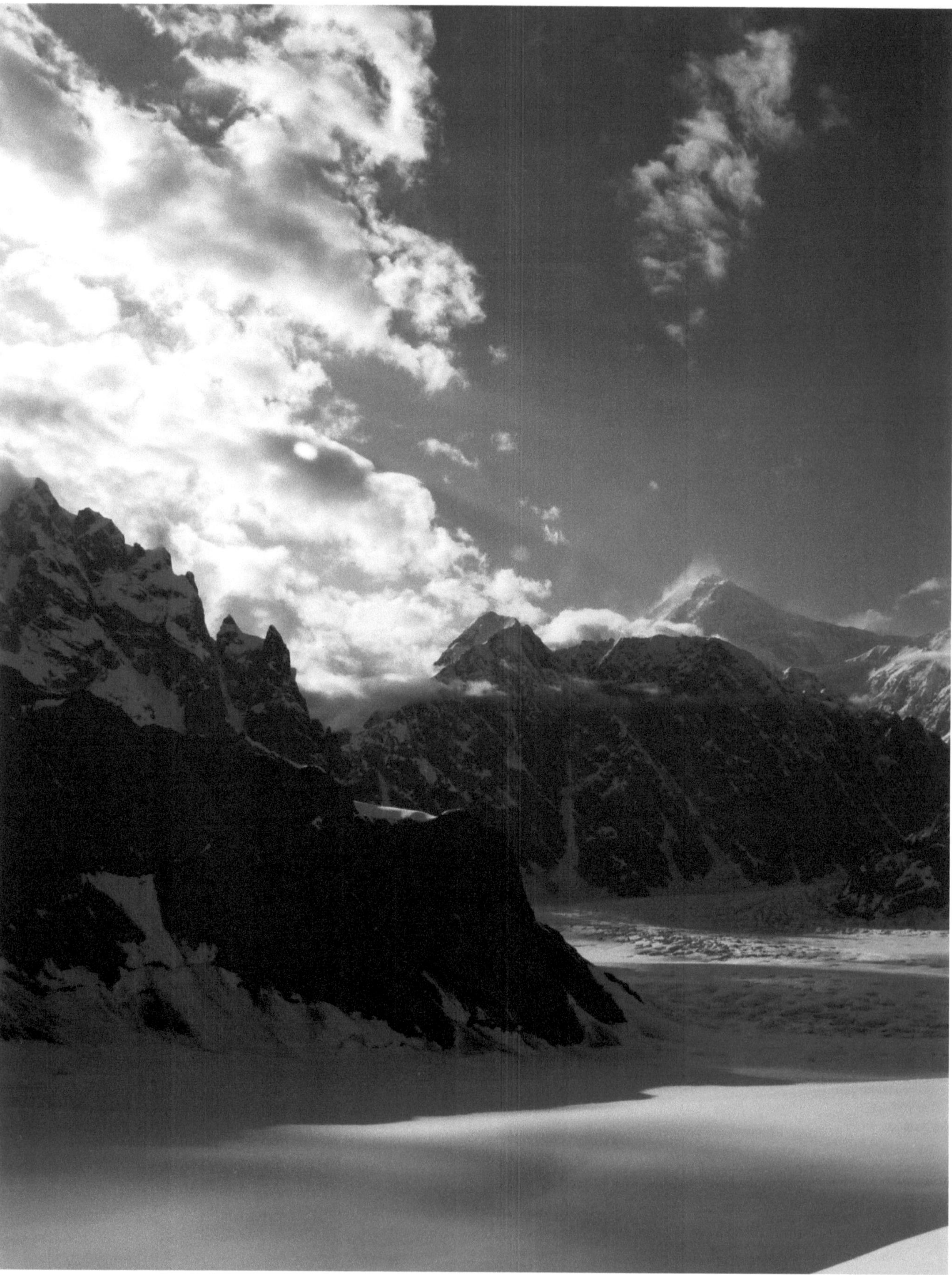

Denali

The sun graced us with his warmth
listening to cracks and crashes
the passage of time
as glaciers move and melt
forming waterfalls
of ice and rock

We raised our glasses
to our dearly departed
"We're closer to heaven here" we said
with hopes that our wishes
would be carried upon
the spiraling breeze
Beyond the Rooster's Comb
and between the Cat's Ears,
to the top of Mount Denali
where she would listen
and in a whisper of Arctic winds
remind them they are not forgotten.

Interconnected

Rooted live wires
crisscross beneath.
These trees that celebrate with me
have sent out the call
to Redwoods three ridges distant
where my feet haven't touched
in years.

And Laurels that remind me
of hot Dogwood canyons
filled with color and song
and dust rising
from dancing feet.

They all know I'm here
and like a rush
all their stories
come racing through the earth.

Madrone before me
shares an Oak's story
of me climbing so high
I could see the ocean
from her outstretched limbs.

And the bracken just laughs
"We've all been here waiting"
Waiting for the day that an open heart
Cracked and mended
Rejoiced in this lightness
That can only be felt
When they've walked in the dark.

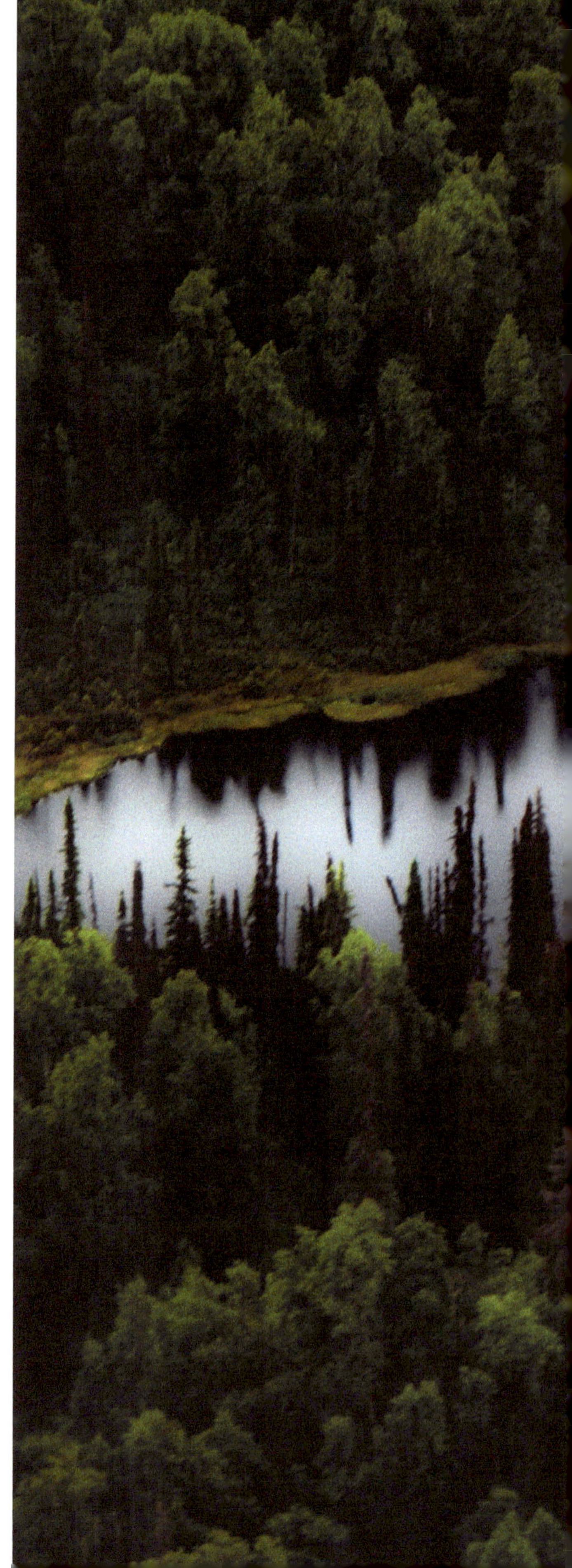

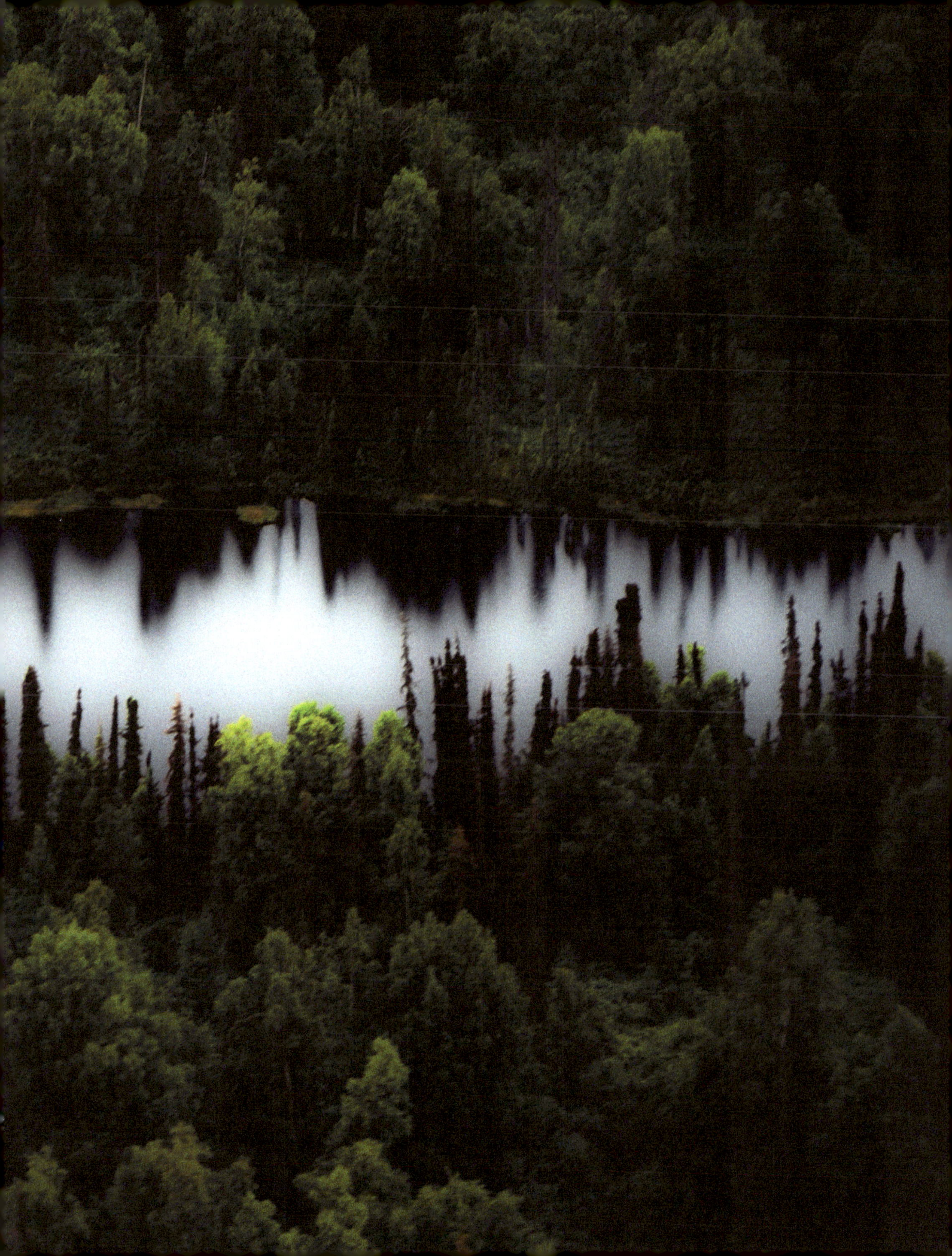

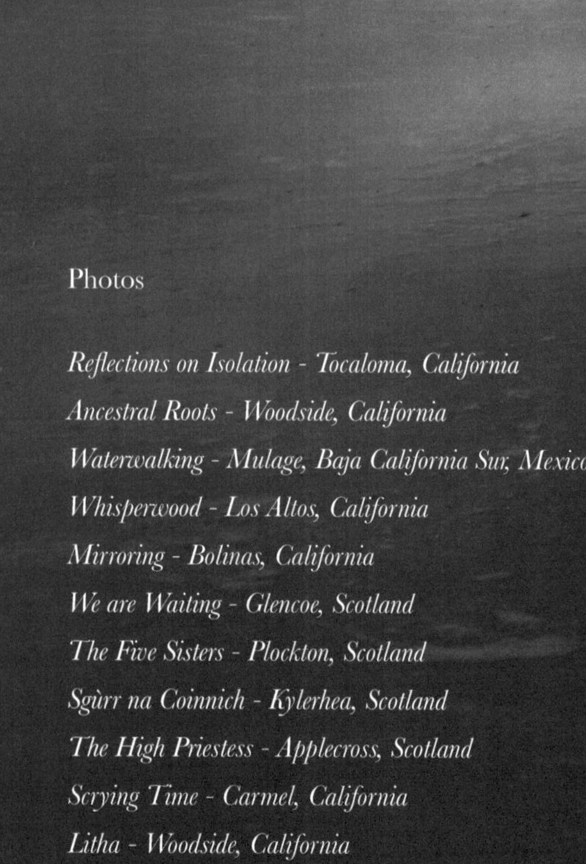

Photos

Reflections on Isolation - Tocaloma, California

Ancestral Roots - Woodside, California

Waterwalking - Mulage, Baja California Sur, Mexico

Whisperwood - Los Altos, California

Mirroring - Bolinas, California

We are Waiting - Glencoe, Scotland

The Five Sisters - Plockton, Scotland

Sgùrr na Coinnich - Kylerhea, Scotland

The High Priestess - Applecross, Scotland

Scrying Time - Carmel, California

Litha - Woodside, California

Metta Mountain - Mount Tamalpais, California

To the Beyond - Point Lobos, California

Rory's Tree - Glen Etive, Scotland

Where the Mist Gets In - Beinn Alligin, Torridon, Scotland

Lovers - Nicasio, California

The Source - Nicasio, California

Beinn na Caillich - Isle of Skye, Scotland

Samsara - Nicasio, California

We Remember - München, Germany

The Cat's Ears Listen - Shelton Amphitheatre, Alaska

Interconnected - Talkeetna, Alaska

The Elephant Sleeps - Nicasio, California

Photo prints available through Rowan and Stone Publishing.
www.rowanandstone.com

Special thanks and gratitude to my Literary Ladies, Juliana, Marlene and Silvana for your support, inspiration and friendship. To Taryn Wieland for your keen eye and editing skills.

To the friends and family who were there - you know who you are. You are loved.

And to my Northman for the hill walk and love that inspired my muse to transmit this project.